WHY BE A CHRISTIAN?

WHY BE A CHRISTIAN?

Ralph Martin

SERVANT BOOKS
Ann Arbor, Michigan

Published by Servant Books
P.O. Box 8617
Ann Arbor, Michigan 48107

Printed in the United States of America
ISBN 0-89283-336-X

90 91 10 9 8 7 6 5

WHY BE A CHRISTIAN?

Why be a Christian? Have you ever asked yourself that question?

You might ask it for any of a number of reasons. Maybe someone has been talking to you about "giving your life to Jesus," and you're wondering whether and why you should. Maybe you come from a Christian background and wonder whether all that religious training you received as a child still has any meaning for you. Maybe you've been trying to live a dedicated Christian life, but lately you've been tempted to give up and you're wondering if it's worth the effort to "hang in there."

Getting to the Essence

I found myself asking the question when I was in college. I had grown up in a good family, a Christian family. As a boy I had a good relationship with the Lord: not that I understood everything about Christianity, but I did think of myself as belonging to God in some meaningful way.

By the time I reached high school, however, I was beginning to wonder whether life at home wasn't a little stifling, whether my parents' views on things—including religion— weren't a little narrow. I wanted to get out, away from home and parents and family, and find out for myself what life was all about. After graduation, I got as far away from my New Jersey home as I could, which turned out to be the University of Notre Dame.

As an undergraduate, my high school questioning grew into full-fledged collegiate cynicism. This was largely because I was searching for the truth, and every alley I turned into seemed to be a blind one.

I started out studying international relations. My plan was to become a career diplomat and work for world peace. I took courses in Russian and political science. But before long I became disenchanted. International relations seemed so petty and superficial: just a long string of crises brought on by greed and treachery and fear and stubbornness.

I decided I needed to get in touch with the deeper human values; literature looked like the realm to investigate. I changed my major and threw myself into investigating the great themes of literature: life and death, love and hate.

By now, I had stopped going to church, and I no longer was looking in the direction of Christianity.

It wasn't very long before I realized that studying literature wasn't getting me to the essence of things. Literature addressed some helpful questions, but it didn't really tackle the *ultimate* questions: What is truth? How can you come to a sure knowledge of it? How can you know that you know? How can you know that you know that you know? To really get to the bottom of things, I thought, I needed to study philosophy. And so I changed my major yet again and immersed myself in the writings of the great philosophers. Two of my special favorites were Plato and Nietzche.

"Why Should I?"

I had walked away from Christianity some time before, but since I was attending a Catholic school people used to ask me occasionally, "Ralph, why don't you be a Christian?" I would always respond, "Why should I? What's the point? Why be a Christian?"

I was given a number of answers. People would say, "You should be a Christian because it helps you be good." To this I could only reply, "Why be good? And what is 'goodness' anyway?" (Philosophy majors are always asking maddening questions like that.) Even aside from those kinds of retorts, I had to wonder what Christianity had to do with living a good, or moral, life. I saw lots of people who were living apparently moral lives, being generous and caring toward others, and they weren't Christians. I even saw people who adhered to other world religions who were living good lives. So what did Christianity have to do with being good?

Other people would say, "You should be a Christian so you can help the poor." But I could see there were lots of people helping the poor who weren't Christians. Any number of government agencies helped the poor. The United Nations helped the poor. If helping the poor was what I wanted to do, I could certainly do it without being a Christian.

Still others would say, "You should be a Christian in order to have meaningful religious experiences, to encounter the Absolute." Again, I wasn't impressed. From what I could tell, having a meaningful religious experience meant sitting in a church, listening to guitar music and hugging people. I could certainly listen to guitar music and hug people, if that's what I wanted to do, without being a Christian. As for encountering the Absolute, I thought I'd rather do it outdoors amid the glories of nature than in a church.

None of the reasons people gave for being a Christian seemed very compelling to me. They seemed to be saying that Christianity was just a means to something else: to personal morality, to social action, to emotional experience. But clearly it wasn't the only means to those ends—and maybe it wasn't even the best means.

God and Group Dynamics

During my senior year in college, I was sharing a room with a graduate student who was a committed Christian and who very much wanted me to be one, too. We had a lot of interesting and heated discussions on the topic.

At one point, Phil invited me to go on a weekend retreat that his Christian group was sponsoring. To humor him, I said yes. I didn't really take it that seriously. The retreat was several months away; by the time it came around we'd probably both have forgotten about it. I proceeded to do just that.

Imagine my surprise, several months later, when Phil burst into our room with an excited smile on his face and said, "Ralph, it's all set! You can go!"

"What's all set?" I asked him. "Go where?"

"The retreat!" he beamed. "This weekend! They've accepted your application! You can go!"

Not only had Phil not forgotten about the retreat, he had actually taken me seriously all those months ago when I had said, off-handedly, that I'd go.

"This weekend?" I said, fumbling for an excuse. "Well, uh, gee, Phil, I mean . . . I couldn't possibly go this weekend. I'm way behind schedule on my senior essay, and my girl-friend is going through a crisis, and . . . well, I'm sorry, but it just won't work."

There, I thought. *That ought to settle that.*

It didn't. Phil began to plead with me. His expression had changed radically. I had never seen him so distraught. "But, Ralph," he said, "don't you understand? You told me you'd go, and I turned in an application for you, and they didn't want to take you because they know how you feel about Christianity, but I talked them into taking you anyway, and now it's all set and you can go and. . . ."

And then I thought I saw some tears. That was too much. My girlfriend and my senior essay would just have to get through the weekend without me. "Okay, okay, okay," I said in exasperation. "I'll go. But I warn you: I am not going to pretend to have a religious experience just to make you happy. I know what's going to happen. You're all going to sit around and sing songs and be nice to each other, and you're going to call it God. Well, I'm not going to call it

God. I'm going to call it clever group dynamics. I'll go, Phil, but I won't sacrifice my intellectual integrity."

The Mind of God?

The retreat went pretty much as I had expected, at least in its social aspects. To my surprise, I found the content of the talks—revelation, salvation, death and resurrection, eternal life—rather interesting. I was especially intrigued by the Gospel of John, which I had never seriously read. As a philosophy student I had read the works of some of the world's greatest minds, and I had to admit that whoever had written the Gospel of John had a pretty impressive intellect.

In fact, it seemed to me that whoever had thought up *Christianity* had an impressive intellect. The uncomfortable thought began creeping into the back of my mind, "Maybe it was God who invented Christianity. Maybe this profound intellect I'm running into here is the mind of God." I tried not to think about it.

I was further intrigued by the way people talked about Jesus. Actually, it made me a little uncomfortable. I wasn't used to hearing people call him by his first name as though he were someone they knew well and chatted with from time to time. I was used to people discussing "the second person of the Trinity" or rattling off the creeds. But these people talked about Jesus as if they had a relationship with him, as if he were a real and regular part of their daily lives. "Either these people are crazy," I thought, "or else they've tuned in to something that I've missed up until now." Somehow I didn't think they were crazy.

In spite of myself, I was actually beginning to find the whole business of Christianity rather attractive. Love, unity, eternal life, cosmic reconciliation, a personal relationship with a wonderful, loving God—these were attractive concepts.

Then they ruined it. They started talking about sin.

"Now, why did they have to go and do that?" I thought to myself. *"Why did they have to start getting negative just when everything was going so well? Just when I was starting to get interested?"*

The worst part was that what they were calling "sin" was what I called "learning experiences." I prided myself on my openness, my "authenticity," my readiness to take in all that life had to offer. Now it appeared that some of my favorite learning experiences fit the definition of sin. These people were suggesting that there were things in my life that weren't loving, weren't right, weren't authentic, weren't true, weren't helpful for me or for others—and I was beginning to see that they were right.

I also prided myself on being an honest seeker after truth. Now I began to see that I had so fallen in love with the search that I couldn't—or wouldn't—let myself find the answer. As long as I didn't find it, there was nothing I had to submit to, nothing I had to conform to, no reality to which I had to relate on *its* terms rather than my own. As long as I kept searching and never finding, I could be my own god.

Searching—or Hiding?

Clearly, something had gotten into my search that wasn't honest at all, a selfishness that wasn't interested in the truth as much as in preserving its sway in my life, no matter what the cost to me or to other people. Under the guise of "searching," I was actually fleeing; under the guise of "seeking," I was actually hiding from the One who was seeking *me*.

I saw all this, and I didn't like what I saw. At the same time, I saw that if what I had been hearing on the weekend were true—if there really was a God who loved me, and who sent his Son to die for me and then raised him from the dead, and who even now was ready to forgive all my foolishness and rebellion and sin, and take me back as his own adopted son—if all that were true, then I had discovered the most important truth that anyone could ever know. I had discovered a teacher more wise than any I had known before. I had discovered a book, the Bible, more valuable than the greatest book written by the greatest human author. I had discovered the key to everything, the source of all life, in the person of Jesus Christ.

By the grace of God, I was able to kneel down at the end of that weekend, repent of my sin, and surrender my life to Jesus Christ. I didn't know what all the implications would be. I didn't know what I was going to do about my girlfriend or my senior essay or my coming graduate studies in philosophy. But I did know that the essence of Christianity wasn't morality, or helping the poor, or religious experience: it was Jesus Christ himself. And I knew that from that time on, my life had to be based on knowing, loving, and following him as Lord of my life.

The Truth of the Matter

Why be a Christian? I'm able to give a much better answer to that question today than I was back in college.

Why be a Christian? Because Christianity is true. In fact, Christianity is *the truth*. It's a revelation of the structure of reality: a revelation of what is, of what has been, of what will be. It's the definitive answer to all those questions of human existence that are so awesome, so mysterious, that we hardly know how to put them into words: Why are we here? Where are we going? How does it all fit together?

Why be a Christian? Not because it helps us be good—although it does. Not because it helps us to serve other people—although it does. Not because it helps us have an experience of God—although it does. The reason to be a Christian is because Christianity is the truth.

Psychologists tell us that the root of mental illness is a refusal to deal with reality on its own terms. If that's true, then the only way to be fully sane is to be a Christian because only in the revelation of God given by and through Jesus Christ are we able to see reality as it is and to deal with it as we must. The only way we can know what reality is, and integrate ourselves into it in a meaningful and fulfilling way, is to discover what God tells us about the universe and our place in it.

Listen to what God tells us through the opening words of the letter to the Hebrews:

> In times past, God spoke in fragmentary and varied ways to our fathers through the prophets; in this, the final age, he has spoken to us through his Son, whom he has made heir of all things and through whom he first created the universe. This Son is the reflection of the Father's glory, the exact representation of the Father's being, and he sustains all things by his powerful word. (Heb 1:1-3)

What a crucial revelation of the nature of reality! It was *through* and *for* the Son that God created the cosmos. It is *by* the Son that the cosmos continues in being. And it is *in* the Son that the cosmos finds its ultimate meaning. Talk about relevance! There would be no universe, no human race, no life, no hope, no meaning at all, if it weren't for the Son of God. If we miss that utterly fundamental fact, how can we possibly understand reality? How can we possibly relate to it meaningfully?

The Structure of Reality

St. Augustine said, "Thou hast made us for thyself, O God, and our hearts are ever restless until they find their rest in thee." We were designed to be in a relationship of love, obedience, and service to God. We will never be fulfilled, we will never know peace, we will never overcome rootlessness and alien-ation, until we find the relationship with God for which we were de-signed. That's the way reality is structured.

The truth of the matter is that we have no lasting dwelling place here on earth. This world is passing away. There's a new world coming, a new age, when Christ returns in glory to judge the living and the dead. Our time on earth is given us so that we can align ourselves with him and be found on his side when he comes again. That's the way reality is structured.

It follows from this that we can't possibly understand reality—we can't hope to make sense out of the world around us—apart from the revelation of God given to us in Christ and through the Holy Spirit.

We can't understand what's going on in the world, what's really important, what forces are really in play, unless God reveals it to us. "Eye has not seen," Paul writes in his letter to the Corinthians, "ear has not heard, nor has it so much as dawned on man what God has prepared for those who love him. Yet God has revealed this wisdom to us through the Spirit" (1 Cor 2:9-10).

The natural man, Paul goes on to say, unaided by God's Spirit, cannot comprehend reality. Only the man or woman who has taken on the mind of Christ, who has embraced God's word in the power of the Spirit, can see things as they really are. We are literally in the dark unless we walk in the light of Christ. We can't see where we're going unless God illumines our path. We're forever trapped in a blind alley unless the Holy Spirit opens a door through which we can see what's real, what's true, what's important.

Why be a Christian? Because life makes no sense apart from Christ.

A Matter of Life and Death

The decision whether or not to be a Christian literally makes a life-and-death difference to each and every one of us. Our very life depends on coming to know Jesus Christ, to receive the forgiveness he offers us, to obey him as his followers.

He himself told us so:

"I solemnly assure you, / the man who hears my word / and has faith in him who sent me / possesses eternal life. / He does not come under condemnation, / but has passed from death to life. / I solemnly assure you, / an hour is coming, has indeed come, / when the dead shall hear the voice of the Son of God, / and those who have heeded it shall live. / Indeed, just as the Father possesses life in himself, / so has he granted it to the Son to have life in himself. / The Father has given over to him power to pass judgment / because he is Son of Man; / no need for you to be surprised at this, / for an hour is coming / in which all those in their tombs / shall hear his voice and come forth. / Those who have done right shall rise to live; / the evildoers shall rise to be damned." (Jn 5:24-29)

There are many things that Jesus says to us in the Gospels, and all of them are important. But some of them are so vital that he calls our attention to them by beginning with the phrase, "I solemnly assure you." It's as though he were saying, "Look, if you don't remember anything else I've said, remember this. Pay attention to what I'm going to say next, because I'm about to tell you something extremely important. Don't miss it. Don't pass it by. It's crucial."

Let's look more closely, then, at what Jesus tells us in this passage.

He tells us that all men and women will rise at the last day and face judgment. On the basis of this judgment, he says, some will rise to eternal life, others to eternal damnation. Who will do the judging? The Son of Man: Jesus himself. On what basis will he judge? On the basis of whether or not we have "done right," whether or not we have heard Jesus' word to us, heeded his voice, placed our trust in God. Don't let it take you by surprise, he tells us. Don't miss this utterly crucial, life-and-death decision: the decision for or against Jesus Christ, the decision whether or not to be a Christian.

Christianity is not a game. It's not a literary theme designed to enrich us. It's not a philosophical puzzle for the intellectually inclined to ponder. It's a cry of love and warning from the God who made us, who sees the desperate predicament we're in because of our own sins, who has gone to incredible lengths to rescue us from that predicament, and who is urgently concerned that we not overlook the only means by which we can be saved.

Why be a Christian? Because Christianity is the truth. Because without that truth, life makes no sense and has no meaning. Because becoming a Christian makes an eternal life-and-death difference to each of us.

True Fulfillment

Once we understand this, we can see how futile are the things that so many people—and perhaps we ourselves—try to live for.

Many people are living for "self-fulfillment," unable to see that there is no fulfillment apart from following Jesus Christ. We weren't created to find complete fulfillment in this life. We were created for eternal life, but apart from Christ, we're cut off from eternal life. We were created for the kingdom of God, but only transformation in Christ can make us able to enter the kingdom of God. We keep trying to find complete fulfillment in this life, but it's not to be found there. It's to be found only in the eternal life that Jesus holds out to us.

Jesus said, "Whoever would save his life will lose it, but whoever loses his life for my sake will find it. What profit would a man show if he were to gain the whole world and destroy himself in the process? What can a man offer in exchange for his very self?" (Mt 16:25-26).

The message of our culture is, "Put yourself first. Look out for Number One. Seek your own way, your own will, your own pleasure, your own fulfillment." But it doesn't work that way. We were created by and through and for Jesus Christ, and apart from him we can have no fulfillment. The only way to save our life is to lose it by surrendering it to Christ. The only way to keep it is to give it away. What good will it do us if we gain all the "fulfillment" this life has to offer, but in the process throw away the eternal life for which we were created?

True Liberation

Many people today are living for causes. "I'm living for justice," they say, or for peace, or for liberation. Their very desire for those things reflects something inherent in having been created by God: without even realizing it, they are hungering for the kingdom of God, where there will be no injustice, no hatred, no strife, no oppression.

But the simple fact is that you can't have the kingdom of God without the King. You can't have peace without the Prince of Peace. You can't have justice without the Just One.

Attempts to establish the kingdom without the King result in man being distorted, in man becoming a god unto himself. Before long he begins oppressing his fellow human beings in the name of the very liberation he strove for!

We can't have liberation without the Liberator. And what we need is not mere political or economic liberation. Our need is for spiritual liberation, for redemption. We need to be forgiven, to be set free from the power of sin, to be spiritually reborn, before we can hope to have justice and peace.

True Riches

Many people today are devoting their energies to the pursuit of "the good life." Their goals in life are success, money, possessions, and status. They dream of boats, saunas, vacation homes, the latest clothes, the finest foods.

Now, I have nothing against all these things in and of themselves, and neither does God. They are all good things. But to make them the focus of our lives, to look toward them to give us happiness and security, is pathetic. Jesus told a story about someone who oriented his life in just this way:

"There was a rich man who had a good harvest. 'What shall I do?' he asked himself. 'I have no place to store my harvest. I know!' he said. 'I will pull down my grain bins and build larger ones. All my grain and my goods will go there. Then I will say to myself: You have blessings in reserve for years to come. Relax! Eat heartily, drink well. Enjoy yourself.' But God said to him, 'You fool! This very night your life shall be required of you. To whom will all this piled-up wealth of yours go?' That is the way it works with the man who grows rich for himself instead of growing rich in the sight of God." (Lk 12:16-21)

It's easy to update the words of the man in this parable. "What shall

I do? I have degrees, and a career, and houses and cars and investments—I've made it. I'm secure. Where am I going to put it all?" Isn't that the mindset that pervades our society? Isn't that the gospel that's preached to us on television and in magazines? Isn't that the ideal that energizes many of us? "Relax! Eat heartily! Drink well! Enjoy yourself!"

But the same words of Jesus provide us with a shock treatment in spiritual reality therapy. "You fool!" he says. That's strong language. "You fool! To draw your happiness and security from those things! To think that those things would last! Why, an earthquake could take those things. A war could take those things. An economic collapse, a serious illness, an accident, an unfaithful spouse, an adverse court judgment could take those things. This very night your life might come to an end. To whom will all this piled-up wealth of yours go then?" Even today, that's the way it works with the man who grows rich for himself instead of growing rich in the sight of God.

Seeing Clearly

It grieves the heart of God to see the blindness and confusion that twist our thinking and turn us away from him. He knows it is our sin that blinds and confuses us; he wants to wipe away our sin and fill us with his Holy Spirit so that we can see clearly and think rightly.

The tragic thing is that all those things that lead us into frustration and despair when we seek them apart from Christ actually *find* their proper place *in* Christ—but we don't see it. In Jesus Christ, under his lordship, everything has its proper place and finds its fulfillment—education, money, politics, sex, everything—because everything has been created through and for him.

Jesus tells us that when we choose to follow him, to make his kingdom the goal and ideal of our life, then all these other things will become ours as well and will take their right place in our lives, working for our good and not for our destruction.

"It is not for you to be in search of what you are to eat or drink. Stop worrying. The unbelievers of this world are always running after these things. Your Father knows that you need such things. Seek out instead his kingship over you, and the rest will follow in turn. Do not live in fear, little flock. It has pleased your Father to give you the kingdom." (Lk 12:29-32)

What a tremendous promise to us from the all-powerful God of the universe! We don't have to make trying to obtain the things we need the driving force or ideal of our life.

Food, drink, clothing, shelter, relationships, jobs, education: the Lord already knows that we need them and already has a provision in store for us. All we need do is get into right relationship with him, seeing ourselves as glad subjects of a loving King, and what we need will come in the right way, at the right time, in the right amount. We need not live in fear because it *pleases* God our Father to care for us in this way. We don't have to take it from him; he *wants* to give it to us.

Why be a Christian? Because it is in relationship to Jesus Christ that we find all life, all love, all joy, all peace, all security, all provision.

The Greatest Gift

Does it seem that it might be too difficult to be a Christian? It won't be. Granted, the initial acknowledgment of our sinfulness, asking of forgiveness, and surrender of self can be a humbling thing. Granted, the daily taking up of our cross and denial of our self can be painful. But whatever pain is involved is nothing compared to the goodness of God that takes hold of our lives. The Psalmist urges us to "taste and see how *good* the Lord is" (Ps 34:9), and Jesus himself assures us that "my yoke is easy and my burden light" (Mt 11:30).

God doesn't want to make our lives miserable; he wants to make them joyful! It's sin that makes life miserable. Scripture tells us that all we get in return for sin is death (see Romans 6:23). It's true: a little sin, a little death; a lot of sin, a lot of death. There is death that comes "on the installment plan," in the heartache and frustration and despair that inevitably flows from life lived apart from God. And there is death that comes at the end, death that never dies, in darkness and gloom and torment, separated from God forever.

"But the gift of God is eternal life in Christ Jesus our Lord" (Rom 6:23). "Do not live in fear, little flock. It has pleased your Father to give you the kingdom" (Lk 12:32). Why be a Christian? Because it's the gracious gift of a loving and merciful, all-wise, all-powerful God. Why not open your heart and receive it? Why live another year, another week, another day, apart from the God who loves you and who is calling you to himself?

Why spend another day trying to build your life on the shifting sands of human wisdom? "Heaven and earth shall pass away," Jesus said, "but my words shall never pass away." His words, his grace, his life, are the only sure foundation. Nations rise and fall; seasons come and go; our own life "is short-lived and full of trouble; / like a flower that springs up and fades, / swift as a shadow that does not abide" (see Job 14:1-2). Life is incredibly short in the context of eternity, and only one thing ultimately matters: deciding to live in and with and for Jesus Christ.

Why Not Now?

Why be a Christian? Because Christianity is the truth, and apart from that truth life can have no meaning. Because Christianity is the source of life and peace and joy, all of which God offers freely to those who acknowledge his lordship. Because being a Christian is what this life is all about; because whether we become a Christian or not makes a life-and-death difference to each of us.

The Lord himself urges you: Don't wait another day. Don't wait another hour. Wherever you are right this moment, whatever you're doing, whatever time it may be, open your heart to the Lord Jesus Christ. Pray this prayer:

Lord Jesus Christ, I want to belong to you from now on. I want to be freed from the dominion of darkness and the rule of Satan, and I want to enter into your kingdom and be part of your people. I will turn away from all wrongdoing, and I will avoid everything that leads me to wrongdoing. I ask you to forgive all the sins that I have committed. I offer my life to you, and I promise to obey you as my Lord. I ask you to release in my life the full power and grace of the Holy Spirit.

Amen.

Other Books of Interest from Servant Books

Let the Fire Fall
Michael Scanlan, T.O.R.

Tells how the Holy Spirit revolutionized the life of Father Mike Scanlan. A bold proclamation of the catching force of the Holy Spirit in the world today, and a testimony to the spiritual truth that all members of the body of Christ can be faithful vessels of the transforming power of God. *$6.95*

Straight from the Heart
A Call to the New Generation
Fr. John Bertolucci

America's best-known Catholic evangelist speaks frankly about the tough questions that young people face today. Encouragement, advice, and solid wisdom to lead you into a deeper and more satisfying relationship with Jesus Christ. *$4.95*

Reflections on the Gospels
Daily Devotions for Radical Christian Living
John Michael Talbot

Approximately four months of daily meditations from the Gospels that reveal much of what motivated John Michael Talbot to abandon all in order to follow Christ and live a simple life, marked by poverty, chastity, and obedience. *$5.95*

CAPTURED

LINDA BARR

ASTONISHING HEADLINES

Attacked	Missing
Captured	Shot Down
Condemned	Stowed Away
Kidnapped	Stranded at Sea
Lost and Found	Trapped

Development: Kent Publishing Services, Inc.
Design and Production: Signature Design Group, Inc.

SADDLEBACK
EDUCATIONAL PUBLISHING
www.sdlback.com

ISBN-13: 978-1-56254-816-2
ISBN-10: 1-56254-816-6
eBook: 978-1-60291-005-8

Printed in the United States of America
15 14 13 12 11   3 4 5 6 7 8 9

TABLE OF CONTENTS

Introduction

A capture can be a triumph, an achievement, or a tragedy. It all depends on the reason for it. In this book, you will read about a runaway slave. He was recaptured just before the Civil War, and was returned to slavery. The debate over slavery tore our nation apart. It was an important time for our country.

Most people are captured because they have committed crimes. During World War II, the Nazis killed millions of people. After Germany lost the war, many Nazis went into hiding. However, their crimes could not be forgotten. People who lost family members wanted justice. Most of the surviving Nazis are now elderly, but they are still pursued—and captured.

Some criminals try to escape after they are captured. Most people thought Alcatraz prison escape-proof. Do you think anyone ever made it out? In Chapter 3, you will find out.

Do you remember the Washington, D.C. snipers? They killed 10 people and held millions hostage. You will read how the police, the FBI, and other groups captured these cold-blooded killers.

Many people thought Saddam Hussein would never be captured. They thought he was too powerful. Yet Saddam was captured without a shot being fired. You will learn how U.S. troops finally found him.

In each chapter of this book, you will learn about an exciting and important capture!

Fugitive Slave Recaptured!

DATAFILE

TIMELINE

1850

Compromise of 1850 sets up the Fugitive Slave Act. Citizens must capture runaway slaves.

1861

The Civil War begins.

1865

The Civil War ends. Abraham Lincoln is shot. Slavery is abolished.

Where are Virginia and Boston?

fugitive - someone who is running away

slave - a person made to work against his or her will; a person who is owned by another

master - in the old South, the boss of slaves

slave state - a state that allowed slavery

free state - a state that outlawed slavery

DID YOU KNOW?

The Mason-Dixon Line was the boundary between Maryland and Pennsylvania. It, along with the Ohio River, was thought of as the dividing line between the slave states south of it and the free states north of it. Washington, D.C. was in the South. Until 1850, Washington, D.C. allowed slavery. It also held the largest slave market in North America.

Chapter One:
Fugitive Slave Recaptured!

The Runaway

Anthony Burns was born as a slave in 1834. However, he was allowed more freedom than most. For example, he could work for other people. He just had to pay his master part of what he earned. Still, Burns wanted to be truly free.

In 1854, Burns worked in Richmond, Virginia. He heard about freedom in the North, so he boarded a ship headed for Boston. He ran away from his master, Charles Suttle.

When Burns arrived in Boston, he sent a letter back to his brother, who was also Suttle's slave. Suttle found and read the letter. Now he knew where Burns had gone. Suttle was determined to get him back.

Back then, Americans had strong— and different—feelings about slavery. Many in the South thought they had a right to own slaves. They needed slaves to work on their large farms. Many in the North believed that slavery was wrong. As more states joined the nation, Congress tried to keep an equal number of free and slave states.

In 1850, California wanted to join the nation. It chose to be a free state. To balance this, Congress compromised. It passed the Fugitive Slave Act. This act said that everyone had to help catch runaway slaves. That even included Northerners.

The Fugitive Slave Act helped Suttle. It required the people of Boston to help him catch Anthony Burns.

Captured!

Like Burns, many slaves fled to the North. Other African Americans living in the North had never been slaves. Yet they were all being hunted down and sent to the South. Many African Americans escaped to Canada. They were not safe anywhere in the United States.

Using the Fugitive Slave Act, Charles Suttle had Burns arrested. The date was May 24, 1854. The arrest shocked the people of Boston.

Burns was held in the federal courthouse. About 2,000 angry people gathered there. They wanted to free Burns. Some charged the heavily guarded building. A deputy was stabbed and died. Still, Burns was not freed. In fact, President Franklin Pierce sent Marines to make sure Burns did not get away.

This poster warns African Americans to avoid talking to watchmen and police officers in Boston. After Congress passed the Fugitive Slave Act, African Americans could be seized and sent south into slavery without a fair trial.

11

Convicted!

On June 2, 1854, a court convicted Burns of being a fugitive slave. That day, he was bound with chains and forced to march from the courthouse to a ship that would take him back to Virginia. About 50,000 people lined the streets of Boston to watch Burns pass. Many yelled, "Shame! Shame!" at the 2,000 troops guarding Burns. The soldiers had orders to fire upon the crowd if anyone tried to free Burns. That day, he was shipped back to Charles Suttle.

It took an African American church a year to raise enough money to buy Burns's freedom. The cost was $1,300, which was a great deal of money then.

Within a year, Burns was back in Boston. Now he was truly free. He attended Oberlin College for two years.

Later, he moved to Canada. Burns became a pastor. In poor health all his life, he died at age 28.

Burns was the last fugitive slave to be recaptured in Massachusetts. Of course, his release was not the end of the story. Slavery was still legal. But the Fugitive Slave Act actually helped end slavery. It forced Northerners to participate in the recapture of runaway slaves. Now slavery affected them, too. As a result, many more Northerners decided to work against slavery. Tensions between the North and the South grew. The nation would be united again only after a bloody civil war.

DATAFILE

TIMELINE

1944
Adolf Eichmann reports to Hitler that 6 million Jews have been killed.

1945
World War II ends.

1960
Eichmann is captured in Argentina.

Where is Argentina?

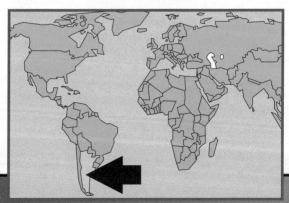

14

KEY TERMS

Gestapo - the German secret police

ghetto - a part of a city where a minority group is forced to live

Avengers - a group that hunts Nazi criminals and brings them to justice

Mossad - an Israeli spy group

safe house - a secret hiding place

concentration camp - a Nazi prison where many people were tortured and killed; death camp

DID YOU KNOW?

Nazis are still fleeing justice. Nazi Maurice Papon was convicted of sending 1,500 Jews to death camps. In 1999 at age 89, he escaped from French authorities.

15

Chapter Two:
Adolf Eichmann Captured!

Proud but Hiding

During World War II, Adolf Eichmann was part of the German Gestapo. It was his idea to collect Jewish people. He herded them into ghettos. Later, he was proud of his role in killing six million Jews.

Before the war, Eichmann tried to become an engineer, but he failed. Still, he was good at organizing things. In 1932, he joined the Nazi Party. There he quickly gained power. By 1941, he was creating death camps. They were the "final solution" to the Jewish "problem."

The war ended in 1945. Germany and Japan lost. Many Nazi leaders were captured and put on trial. Many others escaped. They went into hiding. Eichmann was one of them.

The Hunters

A group called the Avengers formed. It hunted down more than 1,000 Nazis. Still, the Avengers could not find Eichmann. He stayed in Europe until 1950. Then he escaped to Argentina. His wife and children followed him in 1952.

In 1957, the Mossad learned that Eichmann was in Argentina. In Argentina, Eichmann's son found a girlfriend. But he did not know that she was Jewish. The son boasted about his father. He was proud of his dad's role in killing millions of Jews. The son wished that the Nazis had "finished the job."

The Mossad learned where the son lived. They rushed to the Eichmanns' home, but the family was gone.

The Mossad continued to hunt Eichmann. They were worried about catching the right man. All they had were blurred pictures of him. He had left behind no fingerprints. All of the German secret police had a tattoo. However, Eichmann had his tattoo removed.

In 1959, the Mossad learned that Eichmann had changed his name. Now he called himself Ricardo Klement. However, his son kept his old name. The Mossad traced the son to a house in Buenos Aires. At the house, they saw a man who might be Eichmann, but they were not sure.

Then on March 21, 1960, the Mossad watched "Klement" give his wife a bouquet of flowers. Now they were sure. That date was the Eichmanns' silver wedding anniversary.

Captured!

More than 30 Mossad members prepared for the capture. Some of them had suffered in the concentration camps, and many had lost family members in the camps. One man had been part of the Avengers.

The Mossad kept its plans secret from the Argentine police. They knew that the police would think the capture was a kidnapping.

By May 11, 1960, the Mossad was ready. They would catch Eichmann when he returned from work at about 7:40 P.M. They waited outside his house. Two sets of men pretended to fix their cars. They waited as three buses stopped, one by one. Eichmann was not on any of them. Had they missed him?

Finally, a fourth bus stopped. There he was! The agents grabbed Eichmann. They stuffed him in a car where they gagged him and tied him up. Soon they had him back at their safe house. At first, Eichmann denied who he really was, but then he became frightened and nervous. Suddenly, Eichmann was eager to tell all he knew.

The Mossad members were amazed at how ordinary Eichmann seemed. Here was a man who had ordered the deaths of millions of innocent people. Now he just seemed pitiful.

A flight from Argentina to Israel was scheduled on May 20. The Mossad waited until then. If it left earlier than scheduled, the police or government officials might become suspicious.

Justice at Last

After his capture, Eichmann's family looked for him, but they could not call the police. Their Nazi friends were afraid to help because the Mossad was looking for them, too.

To get Eichmann out of the country, the Mossad had a plan. An agent pretended to have an accident. He was taken to the hospital with "brain damage." The agent "recovered" and planned to fly to Israel on May 20. Actually, Eichmann took his place on the plane.

On May 20, the Mossad drugged Eichmann to keep him quiet. At the airport, the agents told the guards that their friend was sleeping because he drank too much. Soon Eichmann was in the plane and on his way to Israel.

In 1961, Eichmann finally stood trial for his war crimes. The trial took place in Israel and lasted from April 2 until August 14. The world closely watched the trial. During the trial, Eichmann sat in a bulletproof glass box. As his terrible deeds were described, people shouted and cried. Some wanted to kill him.

In the end, Eichmann asked for mercy. He begged for understanding. After all, he had only been following orders. The death camps were the fault of the Nazi government.

Eichmann was convicted, sentenced to death, and hanged. The Jewish people were no longer defenseless. They now had their own nation and their own army. They had forced Eichmann to answer for his crimes and his cruelty.

Adolf Eichmann stands trial for his crimes in Israel.

Prisoners in Alcatraz:
Captured or Escaped?

DATAFILE

TIMELINE

1946

Bernard Coy and five others try to escape.

1962

Inmates Frank Lee Morris and two brothers
escape…maybe.

1963

Alcatraz Prison closes after 29 years.

Where is Alcatraz Island?

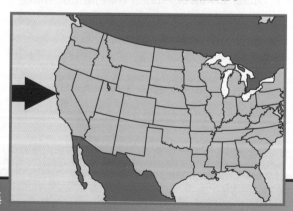

inmate - a prisoner

hostage - someone taken by force to pressure someone else

hostiles - a term used long ago to identify groups of Native Americans who resisted government orders

boarding school - a place where students live while they attend school

privilege - a favor that is granted to someone

warden - the person in charge of a prison

vent - an opening for air

DID YOU KNOW?

Alcatraz Island is now one of San Francisco's most popular tourist attractions. More than one million tourists visit every year, coming from all over the world.

Chapter Three:
Prisoners in Alcatraz: Captured or Escaped?

In the Beginning

Alcatraz was once a bare, rocky island in San Francisco Bay. In 1853, the U.S. Army built a fort on this island. It had a lighthouse. The fort was meant to defend California. However, its cannons were fired at a ship only once. They missed.

By 1861, the island was used as a prison. First, it held Civil War prisoners. In 1898, it held prisoners from the Spanish-American War.

In 1906, a huge earthquake shook San Francisco. Many jails were destroyed. Their prisoners were sent to the island.

In 1912, a cellhouse was built. It was three stories high. By the late 1920s, nearly all the cells were full. The prison became known as "The Rock."

Alcatraz was used as a prison for 29 years. To the inmates, freedom seemed so close. After all, they could see San Francisco just across the bay. The guards patrolled the bay in boats to watch for escapees. Few prisoners tried to leave by swimming. The water there rarely gets warmer than 55 degrees. Fast currents make the trip even harder.

Still, 34 prisoners risked their lives to get away, including two who tried to escape twice. Nearly all of these men were killed or recaptured. A few are still missing. Two groups almost made it. Inmates Bernard Coy and Paul Cretzer led one group. The other group included inmates Frank Lee Morris and brothers Clarence and John Anglin.

The Battle of Alcatraz

Most prisoners at Alcatraz were violent and dangerous. They had been sent there from other prisons. Many had refused to follow prison rules. Some had tried to escape.

At Alcatraz, prisoners had four rights. They could have food, clothing, shelter, and medical care. Everything else was a privilege. Inmates had to work to gain privileges. One privilege was a visit from family members. Another was having a job in the prison.

It took most inmates five years to prove they could be trusted. Only then were they sent to another prison. Some inmates did not wait. They decided to escape. Two of them were Bernard Coy and Paul Cretzer.

Coy had robbed a bank in Kentucky. He arrived at Alcatraz in 1937. Cretzer had robbed three banks. He had also escaped from another prison and killed a U.S. marshal. He was sent to Alcatraz in 1944.

By 1946, Coy and Cretzer had a plan. They invited four other inmates in on it. They would steal guns and blast their way out of the prison.

Coy did manage to get some guns. He also released 24 other convicts from their cells. However, he could not get the key that would let them into the prison recreation yard. Desperate, the gang took nine guards hostage. They pushed the guards into two cells. The Battle of Alcatraz had begun.

Call the Marines!

The prison warden alerted the marines, the navy, and the Coast Guard. The marines rushed the island

and bombarded the cellhouse with mortars and grenades. Navy and Coast Guard boats ringed the island. Thousands of people stood on the San Francisco shore and watched. They heard gunfire from the prison.

Many inmates were trapped inside. They were not trying to escape, but they were in great danger. Some hid behind mattresses.

Bullets flew, and the army threw grenades into the cellblock every half-hour. In time, Coy, Cretzer, and the rest of the gang knew they could not escape, but they decided not to give up. They would fight it out.

Cretzer knew that the hostages could identify him, so he opened fire on them, hitting several. They lay on the cell floor for 10 hours, bleeding. At least one of the guards pretended to be dead, and one did die later.

The fighting lasted two days. Finally, Coy, Cretzer, and another gang member were shot and killed. The other three gang members returned to their cells. They tried to pretend they were not part of the escape attempt. However, all three were caught. Two were executed in 1948. The third one had 99 years added to his prison term.

During the fighting, two guards were killed. At least 18 people were injured. None of the six inmates escaped.

The Great Escape!

Did you see the movie *Escape from Alcatraz*? It starred Clint Eastwood. If you did, you know about Frank Lee Morris and the Anglin brothers. Morris had been in and out of prison his whole life. His first conviction came when he was only 13. His crimes included armed robbery. He was sent to Alcatraz in 1960, after escaping from other prisons.

John and Clarence Anglin were bank robbers. They, too, had a history of escaping from prison. Another inmate, Allan West, helped in the "great escape." He had been sent to Alcatraz twice. West might have planned the whole escape. However, he was not able to leave with the other three inmates.

The four inmates prepared for their escape for seven months. First, they stole tools and supplies. Then they made a raft and life preservers out of more than 50 raincoats and glue. They also made lifelike heads and added human hair from the prison barbershop. They would leave the heads behind in their bunks, along with rolled-up blankets. They hoped the guards would think the inmates were still in their beds.

The inmates also tried using homemade drills to make their cell vent holes larger. However, the drills were too noisy. The men did most of the digging by hand. They also made fake walls to hide their work.

By June 11, 1962, the four inmates were ready for their escape.

Success?

The men planned to leave right after lights-out at 9:30 P.M. Three of them escaped from their cells through their vent holes, but West had trouble pulling his vent out of its hole. Morris and the two brothers climbed up pipes to the cellhouse roof, crossed the roof, and climbed down more pipes to the shower area.

No one ever saw the three men again. By the time West got his vent out, the others were gone.

Later, West explained their plan. They were going to use the raft to get to nearby Angel Island. There they would rest and then swim to the coast. After they stole a car and clothes, the four inmates would go their separate ways.

Did Morris and the brothers really escape from Alcatraz? No one is sure, but the FBI thinks their plan failed. No car or clothing robberies were reported for 12 days after the escape. Two life vests were found floating in the bay. Also, police found a package of letters and photographs belonging to the brothers. They were tightly wrapped to keep them dry.

Several weeks later, a body in a blue uniform was found near the coast. The clothing looked like a prison uniform. However, the body could not be identified. It had been in the water too long.

The three inmates are still missing and presumed drowned. They would have been better off if they had stayed captured!

Alcatraz—The Rock—in San Francisco Bay

Hopi Inmates at Alcatraz

Not only convicts were kept at Alcatraz. Native Americans were sent there, too. The largest group was 19 Hopi "hostiles." These men were sent to prison in 1895. What was their crime? The U.S. government tried to force the Hopis to leave their land. They wanted to give the Hopis new land to farm. The Hopis refused to farm the land that was assigned to them. They—and other Hopis—also would not send their children to government boarding schools.

In fact, the government tried to erase the Hopi language and culture. For example, children at the boarding schools were beaten if they spoke the Hopi language.

So the 19 Hopi "hostiles" were arrested. They were sent to Alcatraz.

The San Francisco newspaper called them "nineteen murderous-looking Apache Indians." Of course, they were Hopis—and not violent at all. The article said the men "are prisoners and prisoners they shall stay until they have learned to appreciate the advantage of education."

The men were kept in tiny wooden cells. Two of them missed the births of their children. The babies died before their fathers could see them.

These Hopis were supposed to perform hard labor until they saw "the error of their evil ways." They were jailed from January 3 until August 7, 1895. After they promised to obey all orders, they were released.

Washington, D.C. Snipers Captured!

DATAFILE

TIMELINE

October 2–22, 2002

Unknown snipers kill 10 people and wound three others in the D.C. area.

October 24, 2002

Snipers Muhammad and Malvo are arrested.

Where were the Shootings?

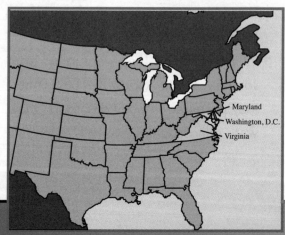

Maryland
Washington, D.C.
Virginia

sniper - someone who hides and shoots at others

wound - to injure

frenzy - great panic or excitement; madness

witness - someone who sees something take place

tarot card - a card used to tell fortunes

DID YOU KNOW?

The police and FBI caught the Washington, D.C. snipers in just 22 days, despite many wrong turns.

Chapter Four:
Washington, D.C. Snipers Captured!

The Shootings Begin

On October 2, 2002, a bullet went through a window at a craft store in Montgomery County, Maryland. It was 5:20 P.M. No one was hurt, and few people paid much attention. No one knew what was coming next—except for two killers.

Less than an hour later, they shot and killed a man in a grocery store parking lot not far from the craft store. At 7:41 the next morning, they shot and killed another man while he mowed some grass. Soon afterward, they shot and killed a cab driver at a gas station. By that evening, three more people had been shot. In all, the killers shot and killed five people on October 3.

By then, the local police were in a frenzy. They knew they had one or more snipers on their hands and had begun to search for them. That same day, the D.C. police stopped a blue Chevy Caprice for a minor problem. They talked to the driver and his passenger. They also checked the car's license tag. They had no reason to keep the men, so they let them continue on their way.

Two hours later, a witness to the last murder of that day remembered something. The witness had seen a dark-colored Caprice leaving the scene. Police started looking for the car. However, the report was too late. The snipers selected their next victim.

Clue from the Killers

The next afternoon, October 4, they shot and wounded a woman in the parking lot of a craft store in Virginia, 50 miles south of Washington, D.C.

On October 7 at 8:09 A.M., they shot and wounded a 13-year-old boy. His aunt had just dropped him off at his middle school in Maryland, not far from Washington, D.C. This time, the killers left a tarot card behind. Written on it was this message: "Mister Policeman, I am God." Police also located the matted grass where the shooter had lain in wait for the victim. There, they found a shell casing from the gun. Both the woman and the boy were lucky. They survived.

The next day, the police found one of the killers, but they did not know it. A Baltimore officer spotted him asleep in his car. It was parked outside a sandwich shop. The officer checked the car's New Jersey plates. He also checked the man's Washington State driver's license. They were both in order. The killer said he was on his way to see his father. After asking for directions, he drove away.

On the evening of October 9, they shot and killed a man while he filled his car at a gas station in Manassas, Virginia. Two days later, they shot and killed a father of six. He had also been filling his car at a Virginia gas station.

More Twists, More Deaths

The police and FBI formed a task force. However, they no longer looked for a Caprice. Witnesses said they saw a white van at the crime scenes. The task force searched for that van.

On October 14, they shot and killed an FBI analyst in the parking garage of a hardware store in Falls Church, Virginia. Some witnesses saw a Caprice fleeing the scene. A man named Matthew Dowdy reported seeing a cream-colored van.

On October 18, Dowdy was arrested. He admitted that he had filed a false report. He had not seen a van leaving the hardware store. False tips like this one made the task force's job even more difficult.

Also on October 18, one of the killers called a priest in Ashland, Virginia. The killer again claimed to be God. He also mentioned crimes in Alabama. Thinking the call was a prank, the priest hung up. He did not report the call to the police.

On October 19, they shot and wounded a man in a parking lot in

Ashland. This time, the killers left behind a letter. It demanded $10 million to stop the shootings. The letter also said the killers had made five calls, including one to the FBI and a priest in Ashland. They complained that no one listened to them. Now they warned, "Your children are not safe anywhere at any time."

Police Close In

On October 20, the police found the Ashland priest. He told them about the call. He remembered that the killer had mentioned crimes in Alabama. The task force thought this might be a clue. They called the police in Montgomery, Alabama. Yes, this town had a shooting much like those in the Washington area. On September 21, 2002, a gunman or gunmen shot two women outside a store. One had died.

The next day, members of the task force flew to Alabama. They were given a fingerprint. Soon they had a name: Lee Boyd Malvo. He was wanted by the Immigration and Naturalization Service (INS). His INS file mentioned a friend named John Muhammad.

The same day, a man called the Virginia police, claiming to be the sniper. The police traced the call to a gas station. There, officers found a white minivan. They quickly arrested the two men inside. They were illegal immigrants, but not the snipers.

The next day, October 22, the snipers shot and killed a bus driver in his bus.

That day, the task force learned that Malvo had lived in Tacoma, Washington. On October 23, they flew there. In Malvo's former backyard was a tree stump. He had used it for target practice. The bullet fragments in the stump matched those in the shootings!

Soon police linked Muhammad to the Caprice that the police had stopped on October 8. Now everyone searched for the Caprice.

Captured!

On October 24, police and the FBI captured both killers. They were found asleep in the Caprice, parked at a rest stop near Frederick, Maryland. In the car was the rifle used in the shootings. The trunk of the car had a hole in it. The hole allowed the killers to lie in the trunk and shoot without being seen.

In December 2003, the killers were brought to trial in Virginia. Muhammad was convicted of one murder. He was given the death sentence. Malvo, 17 years old during the shootings, claimed insanity. His lawyer said that Muhammad, age 42, had brainwashed Malvo. Still, the jury convicted Malvo of one murder. He was sentenced to life in prison. In a second trial in 2004, Malvo was convicted of one murder and one attempted murder.

Malvo and Muhammad killed 10 people in the Washington, D.C. area. They might have killed four more in other states. They also wounded at least three people. The two men kept millions living in fear.

The task force missed opportunities to capture the men. Still, in only 22 days, they found a number of clues. These clues led them to the killers.

Now the killers were behind bars. People living in the Washington, D.C. area could relax at last. Parents let their children play outside again. Gas station customers stopped looking over their shoulders. Business picked up at stores. The community—and the nation—stopped holding its breath.

John Allen Muhammad on trial for murder in the D.C. sniper shootings

Saddam Hussein Captured!

DATAFILE

TIMELINE

July 1979

Saddam Hussein becomes Iraqi dictator.

August 1990

Saddam invades Kuwait.

March 2003

Saddam's regime toppled.

December 2003

Saddam captured by U.S. forces.

Where is Iraq?

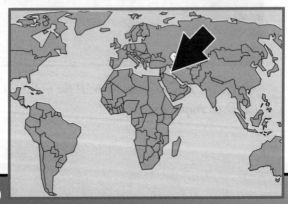

KEY TERMS

regime - a government

peasant - a poor farmer or worker

Baath - a political party in Iraq

coup - a sudden attack to take over a government

Kurds - an ethnic group living in northern Iraq

Shiites - a religious group in Iraq; a member of a branch of Islam

DID YOU KNOW?

Hussein began his political career in 1958. His first act was to kill a supporter of the Iraqi leader who was in power.

Chapter Five:
Saddam Hussein Captured!

Captured "Like a Rat"

U.S. troops searched the farm by moonlight. They were outside Tikrit, north of Baghdad. They had already spent months trying to find Saddam Hussein. The ex-dictator of Iraq was well hidden.

The soldiers poked through a dirty two-room hut. One room had two beds, some books, and clothes. The other room was a messy kitchen. It was stacked with boxes of rotting oranges. Outside the hut, someone noticed a rug on the ground and pulled it back. Underneath, a thick piece of Styrofoam covered a deep, narrow hole. When the soldiers lifted off the Styrofoam, they heard noises coming from deep inside the hole. Then two dirty hands appeared, upraised.

Without firing a shot, U.S. forces had captured Saddam Hussein like a rat in a hole!

At first, the soldiers thought they had found a peasant. Saddam was bearded and dressed in rags. He did not look like a powerful and brutal leader.

It was a surprising end for Saddam. He was born in 1937. As a student, he had joined Iraq's Baath Party. In 1968, Saddam helped plan the coup that brought the Baath Party to power. By 1979, Saddam was the dictator of Iraq. He used fear to control the 24 million Iraqis. Soon he was a leader in the Arab world.

In 1980, Saddam ordered his troops to attack Iran. The war lasted eight years. Hundreds of thousands of soldiers from both nations died. There was no clear winner.

Ruling with Fear

The Iraqis suffered under Saddam. In the late 1980s, the Kurds rose up against him. Saddam dealt with them brutally. Soon, about 180,000 Kurds were missing. Later, mass graves were found. He used nerve gas to kill another 5,000 Kurds.

August 2, 1990, Saddam attacked the tiny country of Kuwait. His forces tortured and killed hundreds of Kuwaitis. They set Kuwait's oil wells on fire. They fired missiles at Israel. They even fired them at Saudi Arabia.

In February 1991, the United Nations stepped in. Troops from the United States and other nations went to Kuwait. Four days later, the Gulf War was over. Saddam withdrew from Kuwait. The United Nations told him to destroy his weapons. He said he did.

Some Iraqis hoped this would be a good time to rebel against Saddam. They were wrong. His forces may have killed as many as 60,000 Shiites and Kurds toward the end of the Gulf War.

In 1992, Saddam drained the marshes in southern Iraq. This drove the people known as Marsh Arabs from their homes. Tens of thousands were arrested or killed. Many just disappeared.

Despite losing the war, Saddam still ruled Iraq. He trusted few people, not even his own family. In 1995, two of his sons-in-law fled to Jordan. Saddam asked them to come back and promised they would be safe. When they returned, he killed them.

Captured!

Then came September 11, 2001. Terrorists struck the United States. Two planes crashed into the World Trade Center. Another hit the Pentagon. A fourth crashed into a field in Pennsylvania. Osama bin Laden said his group were the attackers. He leads a group called Al-Qaeda. Al-Qaeda was based in Afghanistan. The Afghan government protected them.

President George W. Bush sent troops to Afghanistan. After some fighting, a new government took over. It no longer protected Al-Qaeda. The terrorists fled to other nations.

Some U.S. leaders thought Saddam helped with the 9/11 attacks. President

Bush decided to go to war against Iraq. He believed that Saddam had not destroyed his weapons. He thought Saddam would use those weapons against us.

U.S. soldiers invaded Iraq on March 20, 2003. Within three weeks, they defeated the Baath troops, and put the Baath Party out of power. Saddam went into hiding. Over the next months, U.S. forces searched for him. On December 13, Operation Red Dawn began. About 600 troops took part in the raid. They learned that Saddam was hiding near a farm.

The troops searched the farm for Saddam. At first, they did not find him, but then they noticed the rug on the ground.

When they pulled Saddam out of his "spider hole," he was confused. He had a pistol in the hole, but he did not try to fire it. He also had $750,000 in U.S. money.

Saddam on Trial

Saddam spoke to the U.S. soldiers in English. "I am Saddam Hussein," he said. "I am president of Iraq. I want to negotiate."

The soldiers told him, "President Bush sends his regards."

Right after his capture, Saddam was cooperative and talkative. A short time later, however, he was defiant. Iraqi leaders met with him. They told him people were dancing in the streets, celebrating his capture. "Those are mobs," Saddam said.

The leaders asked him to explain the mass graves filled with his victims. "Those are thieves," Saddam insisted.

Saddam was asked about the killing of thousands of Kurds in 1988. He shrugged and said he had heard about it.

Saddam is to be tried in an Iraqi court. He still insists that he is president of Iraq. Eleven of his supporters are also to be tried. Their lawyers say they cannot receive a fair trial in Iraq. Security for the trial will be a problem.

By now, Saddam's trial may be over. You may know the result. However, Saddam is no longer a cruel dictator. Now the Iraqis must try to undo all the harm their nation has suffered.

The Kurds, Shiites, and other groups in Iraq do not get along well. For the good of their nation, they must find ways to work together.

Book Review

Alcatraz Prison in American History by Marilyn Tower Oliver. Berkeley Heights, NJ: Enslow Publishers, 1998.

Would you like to learn more about Alcatraz? This book begins as Alcatraz Island becomes a fort and a lighthouse. Then it describes its years as a prison. The book ends as Alcatraz becomes a national park.

The author tells about many attempted escapes. Learn more about Bernard Coy and his gang. Several people died, but none escaped. Learn more about Frank Lee Morris and the Anglin brothers. They are the ones who tried to escape from the island by using a raft. The author calls their plans "the most daring attempt."

One chapter describes a day in the life of an inmate. The author tells us about some famous inmates. They include Al Capone and Robert "Birdman" Stroud. You can see pictures of old guard towers and a cell. You can also learn more about how the prison was run. Some thought it was too harsh. Others thought these inmates deserved harsh treatment. The prison closed in March 1963.

In 1969, a group of Native Americans took over the island. They wanted the government to help their people. In 1973, however, the island became part of a national park. It is called the Golden Gate National Recreation Area.

This book will help you understand what *captured* meant to the inmates at Alcatraz.

Glossary

Avengers: a group that hunts Nazi criminals and brings them to justice

Baath: a political party in Iraq

boarding school: a place where students live while they attend school

concentration camp: a Nazi prison where many people were tortured and killed; death camp

coup: a sudden attack to take over a government

free state: a state that outlawed slavery

frenzy: great panic or excitement; madness

fugitive: someone who is running away

Gestapo: the German secret police

ghetto: a part of a city where a minority group is forced to live

hostage: someone taken by force or pressure by someone else

hostiles: a term used long ago to identify groups of Native Americans who resisted government orders

inmate: a prisoner

Kurds: an ethnic group living in northern Iraq

master: in the old South, the boss of slaves

Mossad: an Israeli spy group

peasant: a poor farmer or worker

privilege: a favor that is granted to someone

regime: a government

safe house: a secret hiding place

Shiites: a religious group in Iraq; a member of a branch of Islam

slave: a person made to work against his or her will; a person who is owned by another

slave state: a state that allowed slavery

sniper: someone who hides and shoots at others

tarot card: a card used to tell fortunes

vent: an opening for air

warden: the person in charge of a prison

witness: someone who sees something take place

wound: to injure

Index

64